T0338847

A Breathable Light

Rodney Torreson

New Issues Poetry & Prose

A Green Rose Book

New Issues Poetry & Prose
The College of Arts and Sciences
Western Michigan University
Kalamazoo, Michigan 49008

An Inland Seas Poetry Book

 Inland Seas poetry books are supported by a grant from
The Michigan Council for Arts and Cultural Affairs.

First Edition, 2002.

ISBN   1-930974-23-X (paperbound)

Library of Congress Cataloging-in-Publication Data:
Torreson, Rodney
A Breathable Light/Rodney Torreson
Library of Congress Control Number: 2002104237

Art Direction   Joseph Wingard
Design   Michael Green
Production   Paul Sizer
                  The Design Center, Department of Art
                  College of Fine Arts
                  Western Michigan University

A Breathable Light

Rodney Torreson

New Issues

WESTERN MICHIGAN UNIVERSITY

Also by Rodney Torreson

The Ripening of Pinstripes: Called Shots on the New York Yankees

for my mother and father, Don and Vicky
also for my sister, Kathy
and my brothers, Dean, Bill, Tom, and Rich

and for Kathy Drzick

Contents

III.

I.

How Deer Reveal What You Are

Two deer
carve everything
they show themselves against:
tree, fence, slope of sky—

You the intruder
to a place
you lived half your life.

Until now you never saw
corn rows for what they are.
The deer turn
their bodies so head and hind
peer at you, each brown stalk
working up to the power
of a torch
to find you somewhere
past wordlessness.

Fiona Pruess: Feelers

From among the pansies and azaleas
he slipped so close
his beard grazed her arm
through the window screen
where it lay on the sill that limp
summer night while she watched TV:
an insect she was about to
slap. He crawled her arm,
small, impervious, loose
from his own life,

crept the round of her shoulder, skirting
her blouse. A small rush.
She felt him again, up under her chin,
slapped him across his pupils
stretched to their limits, cried out
as he shrank back into
the wild summer colors dimmed only
by the dark working hard in the shadows.

In the week toward corn harvest,
he had a part in everything beautiful.
Even she could see his eyes:
in every window, beneath her bed,
in the feathered glances
of neighbors,
exotic, more brilliant
than a peacock's fan.

Visceral Dust

On rear legs a stallion
parses motion, stamping hooves.
The wind gallops; the horse heaves
into the gallop its form.

Sows come back, upturn
baskets of corn, but first their snouts
rout out the dead fences
as if part of the bargain
were to raise them from the ground.

Branches, dragged across our trails
to say we've never been,
upright themselves, leaf into
towering sprawls, stones turn
in the corners of fields.

Our new bodies not far behind,
a visceral dust rises to meet us,
waving us over to lighted eyes.

Before Sleep Was Savage to What Might Have Been

we slipped past
the last temporal things,
a squeaking cemetery gate
complaining, perhaps,
that we were too alive,
showing off among the dead—
you, too beautiful, as if a lie
for the sake of the poem,
laughing among stones
which barely held down eternity,
you wherever I would touch,
as we played tag
on our fingertips.

It meant nothing when a bee,
that dark brow furrowed
about an eye,
darted upon you madly.
We knocked it off
in a rinse of silence
smudged face to face,
skittish.
You said you didn't
want to be famous.
Then a kiss became a quandary.
I took you into a smile
that drew to your eyes
sparks of an ancient fire,
the mounds not mown,
the winds restless about staying.

The Wind Out Here

is our wind,
this breeze just waking,
shrugging off two days
of dust, then washing clean
across the bean rows,
where you hoe cocklebur.

You welcome the wind
by taking off your cap.
In an instant
it sets on your head
the common man's crown—
crystals of your own sweat—
and, no respecter of fences,
gives you land to the horizon.
No, not to own but in the sovereign spin
of that moment
in the dry Iowa wind,
a stirring sings in you
a leafy consciousness.

The Trees No Longer Scintillate

under a spirit glaze of ice.
It's been weeks now
since they stemmed the last bright stars,
their trunks now drab
as old trash cans and rain barrels,

each patch of snow
high on a branch
no hand of assurance.

When we notice them again,
a leaf or two
has put each limb at peace,
a green sprig here and there
in our own heart season.

Something leans, slopes
toward home, a shivering branch
from our matching moon.

Where Weeds Wander to a Height of Fitful Sleep

your hand parts them, about a half mile
into the pasture, at the dredge ditch,
to find your next step.
Suddenly a colossal shell
with a winding stair,
a shell translucent enough
to see why a tree bough
bends on the other side
or a hill settles for being a hill,
where reason makes
the season turn at its boldest touch,
a snail shell twenty feet tall,
every whorl a crawl space
you move through
to find what you find
when you give up
what is searched for.
How small we are heading home,
how much of everything
and everyone we've become.

Girl in a Hammock

Hidden in this pod, a romance novel
perched high in her hand—then the dangling leg,
dark mole on her thigh, this exotic something
from the other side, the boy on the lawnmower mowing.

The rest of the girl doesn't have a clue
that this precocious leg has left its twin—
to swim into the mind of the boy—
every romance novel unfinished
for a leg to feel out an ending.

Taillights of the Thunderbird

In the turn-off to the pasture,
the couple whirling in skin
as if from one's mouth
was born the other's head.

Yet the glow of the taillights
outdoes them, as weeds
and sedan grass,
forth and back,
spring more
than water reflections
recede a fence.

Not a soul sees these lights
whisk them to the wilds,
no one but the boy, always somehow
in back of what happens,
like a ditch sleeper
who awakens to weeds
that strum a song
across the body, their reach
now too far beyond the farm,
the world spanned in lights
wired to weeds
and what the heart leaves there.

These Parts Don't Take to Strangers

seen first through the head eyes
of cars stooping
to country roads late at night.
Or maybe it's just a map light on
in the turn-off to a pasture.
Somebody reads the map
of your palm across four fences
interspersed with alfalfa, corn,
and the limited field
of your future tracked
in the crunch of tires
you'll take in your cereal
if you live until morning,

the sniff of him saved in
wild strawberries along the ditch
which open their pores
to breathe in his smells.
He pokes headlights into
the lane, out again,
looking for something,
then beams off again,
as if he is gone, but now
a wide sweep around the yard,
the shiny sedan flashing,
his perfect teeth
encapsulating light.

Eyelashes Spider Her Cheeks

Then the girl wakes among weeds
of old machinery when a cottontail leaps
past golds and yellows
of a rusty planter, precursor to the fall.
She follows. Metal cracks slowly into leaves
nearby a thresher and small-throne tractor;
in the distance she can see a stray house—
yesterday's life sewn shut by hanging boughs.

The rabbit nears a snare of brush.
Her mother's life. She follows the hare
among old bottles and cans
that poke up from the past. Across the fence
she hears soybeans breathing
in slow undulations. Weeds wear her down
as the rabbit springs left and she follows
in the newest models of light, knowing
this is her time. Her bare legs sing her song,
the way they catch the dew.
She knows there are secrets here,
like the garter snake in the grass
creeping against everything she believes,
where the creek ravines into her and hills swallow.

She tries to corner the hare, catch it somehow.
In months to come, here will lie pure, heaped snow
where a loader has dumped the whiteness
over and through. If she can catch it and not let go,
hold it and nothing new ever under her blouse.

II.

On a Moonstruck Gravel Road

The sheep-killing dogs saunter home,
wool scraps in their teeth.

From the den of the moon
ancestral wolves
howl their approval.

The farm boys, asleep in their beds,
live the same wildness under their lids;
every morning they come back
through the whites of their eyes
to do their chores, their hands pausing
to pet the dog, to press
its ears back, over the skull,
to quiet that other world.

In Winter after Father Lost His Hand in the Combine

The brooder door ajar,
the chickens,
as if to mock
the unwielded axe,
strutted into the snow
as though they had laid
their first abstraction.

They shook their combs
at the only words
they understood:
in a gust of feathers
flung themselves
upon the drifts
where they floundered.

The cold composed them
but in the morning
their only clear point
was at the end
of their foolish beaks.
Mother found them
frozen stiff, claws caked
to the branches
where they perched
in the trees,
eyes glazed
as if on the verge
of getting it right.

Child, Know

how a little hole
swallows a wall,
the metal trigger
of a mousetrap tailing
when we carry it.

Butter up a small death;
it will not shock us then,
the mousetrap
a passageway to home.

A little cheese, please,
for the corners,
under furniture, the fuzz of fur
on the register,
a metal grating, child.

Put your finger in there.
The mouse gnaws
on the chicken bone.

How a Cat's Slink

will rasp indifference
against
the barn door,
lengthen
the cat in
at milking time.

But when
the boy slants a teat,
the feline, upright—
abandonment leaps
to the pleasing shock
of a string
whitely drawn—

this only tether to
ever bind it,
the cat swallows
until the boy, too,
is gone—
his mind field-blown,
and the cow
a mere tuft
of forgetfulness.

Under the Yard Light

Where car lights follow
the gravel's curve,
I see the flexing shadows
of fences.

Mother says I may never wake.

I think the circles
my life makes
are accidents:
glass marks on the dresser.

Cattle stretch
their necks toward the sky
and try to say *moon*.

The Fear of Tornadoes

When she awakes,
the air seems too alive, the fan
finally amounting to something.
She's in fragments:
part of herself in every bed.

She wonders, Does the hub of worry
in her forehead
add spin to the fan?
There's too much breeze
unaccounted for.

She holds her breath,
pulls the plug,

and there's not enough wind
to turn a leaf.

Before she rushes to the basement,
she pulls on arms,
dresses herself in children.

In the Dark Where Clothespins Set the Wires to Notes

Pole to pole the dried wash
leads to a cleaner sound
than one could suppose—
the wind through the window screen—
as mother, trying to sleep,
worries the school clothes to order
and dreams the wind, like Harpo Marx,
turns the clothesline vertical,
a harp between its knees, to pluck
a promise the crops shall be
wandered through by rain,
the wind's feet pedaling,
"Hurry up, hurry up."

Riding the Barn

You straddle the ridge of the roof
with the weathervane
arrowed up,
your heels nudging in
where your thighs gather
the rafters and mow.
Even the homelier cattle pen
and stanchions,
the oat bin and horse stall
tell you it's come to this—
a shiver filled up
with the farthest stars—
something about being up there
without knowing how
you arrived,
and no chance
of ever coming down.

After I Swung That Leather Throne

saddled the stallion, letting
those lordly footstools
of stirrups hang,
I'd mount my work.

How I'd fear the cinch
was no cinch;
if a horse had room
to breathe his pasture in,
the saddle would
slide down, carry me,
clinging, riding the horse's belly,
my boots digging upward.

The spooked horse would
muscle into pasture,
my head striking the
grassy sky until I saw stars,
my hands straining
after the legs,
those reins, trying
to skirt clouds,
that scuttle of stones,
lean in,
pray my head gallop.

Pig Train

Through the dark birth canal
a train of pigs, the engine
of a snout, the first wreck
a bloody one into
straw. Where tracks end
abruptly, cars pick themselves
up from a glistening
shake-up in the afterbirth,
no whistle but squealing
and plenty of steam.

Farmyard Gate

In a turn of wilderness
it was born.
Decisions were easy
in the swing of it.
But now, with the boy
hitching it beneath his arm,
it has slowed down,
as if to ponder grass,
its plans sprigging
here and there.

And what does this mean
to a gate
more often open, perhaps,
than closed to things?—
the boy of it just a post
driven into mud
by his own weight.

Doing Chores in the Dark

Doing chores,
I had no good reason,
my father insisted,
for fearing the dark,
but that evening
a tractor drove itself
crazy, choking
and coughing over
the ruts, around
the oat bin and crib,
delirious with lights.
I had, that moment
before dropping my pails
to head for the house,
all the reasons I needed
for running.

In a Hummingbird Light

The nimble dawn,
a lamb
gumming a bottle with a rubber teat,
biting it, fighting for the sum
of a drop.
The lamb's heart
beating wings a thousand times
while the bottle
at the end of its nose
is some silly beak,
his woolly cord
slapping the short sidewise sky.
You hold him back, pat down
his bounce, this orphan
bucking the bottle.
The squeeze hole opening up,
the lamb thrusts off
his front hooves, flying back,
then forward, a fragile instant
held hard, flowering
the electric pulse that is morning.

Dusk, the Middle of Burr Oak Lake, Two Brothers Leap One Ice Slab to Another

barely elude that other marvel—
plummeting through—

then leap again,
as if reading themselves
into the dreams of trees,
believe they grow to be
lightning.

It's later, long after
they laugh short
the inexhaustible depths
that they stand, feet drenched,
belaboring shadows,
until jostled by a loon passing
they lunge headlong.
Hammered knees
catch a solid piece;
beyond it, nothing.

For minutes, they stare,
then one brother
sees on the lake
a whirring moon.
The other breathes
one leap beyond it
a girl's face
he dreamed of while milking,
when a skewed stream
had him imagining
her hair about
his shoulders, belonging there.

The moon and girl's face
become ice,
as nature meant them,
the feet finding a way
where the heart stops.

The Song

The cow's tail lashes
the flies out of rhythm.
But the teats drive the song.
And it is through
milk the lane streams,
the creek casts
over stones;
even apples spill
in the rhythm
silking the pail.

Fences

Sometimes his fences
seemed so frail
and fixing them so hard.
The farmer had sons,
but they weren't
the mending type. They were
for slipping out themselves
through any thing
he'd devise. He *could*
hit them with
the post-hole digger
and make them mind.
But having the ones
who break fences mend them
seemed a failure
from the start,
so the boys slipped south
of the farm with
a whiskey jug,
and before another moon
cracked open
they were joined by
heifers crossing
over in front.

Pilgrimage

His uncle's shirt in a hand-me-down slide
arrives. Now he's wearing it,
holes in the elbows leaving room for God.
Yet the empty machine shed
on a day he is young
collapses when he looks at it.
Dust puffs the shed up again,
but it disintegrates in wind.
On the barn floor,
straw tries
to burn its own sun,
possessions look back toward their maker.

No spices but milk, a teeming pail
with whiteness never tainted
though he walks for years.
Grass which clung to the udder
sticks to the pail,
stems the wind picks loose, gusting them up
onto the star he will follow.

Through time swatted like flies
he grows older,
and the waves of milk shiver
on his coarse, unapologetic hands.
When he closes his skin at night,
his eyes are open beneath the lids,
his lungs feasting on a breathable light.

III.

After the Midnight Train Rumbles through Staples, Minnesota

you hear it, almost moth-like
on the porch screen,
all that's left
of the Burlington Northern,
a tremble in the mesh,

imagine the whistle
feathered into antennae,
everything from engine to caboose
collapsed in a body
too faint to discern,

and wings, small as the
flickering thought
of a weary dispatcher
in a city too far from here
to matter.

At the Old Rodeo Site by the River

for Marcie Frevert

Each summer a horse or two glistening with sediment
and pulsed, perhaps, by tremors
of a tractor pull, surge
from the riverbed—
broncos red at the flanks
as if they'd called upon
the kingdom of fish to fin them,
make blood a sign for boot heels
to keep their bite.

Locals, slow to avow these horses,
spot them bucking in the oats,
forming crop circles
where they and riders
forty years earlier
coiled from chutes.

Before someone can ponder
rounding them up,
trucking them off
toward sale barn or science,
the broncos' knees collapse beneath their weight,
breath slumping in a heap.
But first, heads nod
and hooves stamp
as if in the bucking
differences with this age
might yet be worked out.

No Seedlight, But an Itch in the Oat Bin

goes back to the beginning, past
the name of Lars Waldee, the builder
of this barn in 1907, a name
itching to be remembered,
who lives off the meager
rations of his scrawl, which
father's flashlight held
an instant on this black expand-
ing wall before the wall slipped

farther back, where, darkly
apprising himself of
himself, God's spirit,
chaff-driven and brooding,
scratched an astounding itch to
create the first man: and
here you are, the oats
of origin sown into your socks,
waiting for a world to begin.

The Farmer's Clothes Are Hung in the Utility Room

a seed corn cap, behind it
straps hang down to overalls, boots.
Unpeeled is a man cattle and hogs
would not recognize. Bald of cap,
he rolls up his sleeves,
bends over the sink, washes
the fields from his arms,
hand, and stump, onto the field
of the washcloth,
the lower forty by the dredge ditch
he scours from his face, drops
into a pan beneath the sink,
the whole farm summed up
in the towel he drifts over arms,
face, ears, behind them,
the rib of cartilage.
A father eating supper
with a bread slice
wipes up the last of his food,
fades into the couch
until the goodnight kiss
on his cheek brings him back.

Picking Rock the Day Martin Luther King Was Slain

Odd chunks we cast upon the load,
ungainly, broken down, heavable bone
from the earth's core. But frost levered in
among gray slabs, pummel pounded out
on the glacier anvil, askance
protuberances, all kinds of blind fathomings
rearing up, some you could not quiet,
pry from the soil, lug to a corner of the field.

It, Too, Does What It Must Do, This Sparrow—a Stick Fixed through It

a torrent of protruding wood
from breast and back.

Along the briar, it sweeps
an encumbered curve, climbs
the scaffold of a feeder,

hammering a beak,
building a future

not down the middle
of this still life: a twister
but to each side

while never sensing
how a man has poised
on both ends of that stick
in the smallest pails
parts of a life—
his own mortar.

Variations on a Farm Garage at Night

1.

Out where a sawhorse coarsens
the shadows, jagged tooth saws
in varied lengths of elation,
a workbench with vice, that lone bicep,
clenched around a plowshare.
On the tool bench a mower blade
saluted by shiny sickles;
hanging hammers, screwdrivers,
and crescent wrench
reach for the last time they were used;
underneath, a spilled sky of screws.

2.

In a corner a post-hole digger
and metal pod of a planter;
storm windows dressed in the dust petals
of last year's rain. The grease gun,
out of place, has drawn the letter *I*
on the concrete floor; upstairs
cobwebs map a big wheel-grinder
run by a foot pedal, an old dresser
and mirror; on a desk dusty with purpose
Horatio Alger books are piled to a sneeze,
the smart knickers worn again
to threads on the cover. Steps back down
to stalls for two cars, one with
plumped corn sacks that seed
mice tracings; in the other
sockets where headlights, holed up
an instant in the wall, are turned out,
the car keyed to a sigh
that settles everything into memory,
the slow echoes of voices, once ours.

Locker

Heaving before him
the thick door of the meat vault,
the butcher, abreast with slabs
and boulders of meat.

Aproned he strides,
as spirits, or other aprons, wisp about,
tying themselves to him,
his blue eyes still marbling
into neat wreckage a ham, perhaps.
Nothing up front
but the counter,
this antithesis
of physician.

Through the door
crude wreaths
of trimmed fat and gristle
in memorial, and poised
in still breath a cold passion
equal to smoke.

All Afternoon the Distances Feel Good on Him

this farmer,
whose silence is a fence
others climb;
even grass lunges
up a wooden plank,
his pauses,
unencumbered now
by words,
wear smooth.
The prairie does
this: chaff separates
from grain,
as words do from
a man, leaving him
to bear a passage
through his family,
trail light
in the middle
of his years,
his fears sleeping
like clouds
caught on nailheads
in the barn,
his footsteps woven
among small talk
without touching it.

Daylight Deepened the Argument

Then he killed her.
They looked through him
for evidence of morning.

But he was evening now,
shackled to stars
which strung along his wife
and a myriad of
the calmest excuses,
a heart clean again,
shooting through
in chest hair near
his collar, brazenly pure.

He was field-blind now
from a whole day's work
of tilling soil.
He had made his mercy
against legs poking
from behind a freezer.

Didn't spring plowing
prove his future?—
tumbling, turn-
ing a fresh furrow—
a black one, then another
until blue sky, alone,
bruised her,

until murder was rows
behind, across
the fence,
in some other field,
an abstract notion
worked out long ago
in his hands.

At the Communion Rail of Walnut Lutheran Church

Maybe every street in Graettinger
runs through you, manhole covers
numbered 1941,
your heart on the floor,
head in your hands, the stained glass
ribbed like a leaf, God rough enough
to find you where you are.
Planes of wood rise crosswise
from your back. Maybe hope
crawled over the hill—
your pulse so thin it is God's wafer.
Perhaps you're beaten down
by farm loans, doors you must
continue to open,
or you have worked the dark
out of your own hands, fleeing
through the burning cornfields,
returning to see
the kids off to school.
Perhaps hunted by thick-lensed men
who scrutinize the wings of a signature,
you gulping the silence—
an opening in the fence.

After Many Winters the Rooted Stairs
of the Cellar Call

He is silent:
the moon has his howl.

He slides down
broken stairs, bandages
of crumbling cement
among mildew and toadstool.

At the empty thread-spool,
the humblest doorknob,
he slips through
to where she is waiting,
her soul now orchestral,
with the moon in his hand.

The Bethlehem Nursing Home

A birdbath ministers
to the lawn chairs,
all toppled: a recliner
on its face, metal arms
trying to push it up;
an overturned rocker,
curvature of the spine.
Armchairs on their sides,
webbing unraveled.
One faces the flowers.
A director's chair
folded, as if prepared
to be taken up.

A Few Sleepy Towns out of Sioux Falls, South Dakota

he'll ponder how
through his hospice pillow
the bird of his song
this morning
poked him with a feather,

the raising of its wing
his opening eye.

And how on the falling side
of midnight
he was blinking hard,
swooping a winding blacktop
for the rig
he's now driving,

his freight
towed by headlights,
sunflowers beaming him
toward a truck stop
for coffee.

Before he lofts it
toward his lips,
he'll gaze down into
that bird's
dark eye.

Windmill

Cattle and hogs awash in the sky
propel with their hooves
the broken farm,
on the wheel's underside
as well, livestock scamper
upside down, having returned—
spirits won over by slaughter.

The old farmer and wife
set down their bones,
join in with a vigor
not seen in years,
making a treadmill of
radiating sails
now surging through the sky
where birds don't fly anymore,
where the cistern door's
peering eye rises,
brothers and sisters
though still in their skins, join in
a second run-through of their lives.

Landscape with Trees

by George Elmer Browne, American (1871-1946)

How the human spirit,
clothed in trees, eases
the ache of eternity,
rises above the roots
that ruled here. For the trees
pull even this dirt road up.

Before the storm clouds settled out,
we were lost on a journey.
Released from our shoulders we leave
behind that laggard, our bones,
leased before we were born, in the shadows
as roots give us flight,
and we surge through the trunks
beyond the hill rippling leaf to leaf.

Acknowledgments

Grateful acknowledgment is made to the editors of the following journals, magazines, and anthologies in which these poems first appeared, some in different versions:

Cape Rock: "The Bethlehem Nursing Home"

Contemporary Michigan Poetry: "After the Midnight Train Rumbles through Staples, Minnesota"

Controlled Burn: "The Trees No Longer Scintillate"

Cottonwood Review: "Doing Chores in the Dark"

Dry Creek Review: "Where Weeds Wander to a Height of Fitful Sleep"

Hiram Poetry Review: "No Seedlight, But an Itch in the Oat Bin"

Louisville Review: "Pig Train"

Parting Gifts: "Fiona Preuss: Feelers"

Pinyon: "In a Hummingbird Light"

Poet Lore: "All Afternoon the Distances Feel Good on Him"

Potpourri: "How Deer Reveal What You Are"

River City: "At the Communion Rail of Walnut Lutheran Church"

The Small-Towner: "In Winter after Father Lost His Hand in the Combine"

Sou'wester: "On a Moonstruck Gravel Road"

Studio One: "Eyelashes Spider Her Cheeks"

Willow Review: "Daylight Deepened the Argument," "A Few Sleepy Towns out of Sioux Falls, South Dakota"

The Windless Orchard: "Under the Yard Light"

"The Fear of Tornadoes" first appeared in *On a Moonstruck Gravel Road,* a chapbook issued by Juniper Press.

"Landscape with Trees," commissioned by the Grand Rapids Art Museum, first appeared in *Poetry and Painting in the Galleries.*

Sincere thanks to Miriam Pederson and Russell Thorburn.

I would also like to acknowledge David Allan Evans—specifically for his poem "Uncle Claude," which was my inspiration for "After the Midnight Train Rumbles through Staples, Minnesota."

photo by Mikel Cahill

Rodney Torreson, after growing up in Iowa, moved with his wife Paulette to Grand Rapids, Michigan, where he teaches at Immanuel-St. James Lutheran School. He and Paulette have three children: Tasha, Ted, and Travis. In addition to *A Breathable Light,* he is the author of *The Ripening of Pinstripes: Called Shots on the New York Yankees,* published by Story Line Press.

New Issues Poetry & Prose

Editor, Herbert Scott

Vito Aiuto, *Self-Portrait as Jerry Quarry*
James Armstrong, *Monument In A Summer Hat*
Michael Burkard, *Pennsylvania Collection Agency*
Anthony Butts, *Fifth Season*
Kevin Cantwell, *Something Black in the Green Part of Your Eye*
Gladys Cardiff, *A Bare Unpainted Table*
Kevin Clark, *In the Evening of No Warning*
Jim Daniels, *Night with Drive-By Shooting Stars*
Joseph Featherstone, *Brace's Cove*
Lisa Fishman, *The Deep Heart's Core Is a Suitcase*
Robert Grunst, *The Smallest Bird in North America*
Robert Haight, *Emergences and Spinner Falls*
Mark Halperin, *Time as Distance*
Myronn Hardy, *Approaching the Center*
Edward Haworth Hoeppner, *Rain Through High Windows*
Cynthia Hogue, *Flux*
Janet Kauffman, *Rot* (fiction)
Josie Kearns, *New Numbers*
Maurice Kilwein Guevara, *Autobiography of So-and-so: Poems in Prose*
Ruth Ellen Kocher, *When the Moon Knows You're Wandering*
Steve Langan, *Freezing*
Lance Larsen, *Erasable Walls*
David Dodd Lee, *Downsides of Fish Culture*
Deanne Lundin, *The Ginseng Hunter's Notebook*
Joy Manesiotis, *They Sing to Her Bones*
Sarah Mangold, *Household Mechanics*
David Marlatt, *A Hog Slaughtering Woman*
Gretchen Mattox, *Goodnight Architecture*
Paula McLain, *Less of Her*
Sarah Messer, *Bandit Letters*
Malena Mörling, *Ocean Avenue*
Julie Moulds, *The Woman with a Cubed Head*
Marsha de la O, *Black Hope*
C. Mikal Oness, *Water Becomes Bone*
Elizabeth Powell, *The Republic of Self*
Margaret Rabb, *Granite Dives*
Rebecca Reynolds, *Daughter of the Hangnail; The Bovine Two-Step*
Martha Rhodes, *Perfect Disappearance*
Beth Roberts, *Brief Moral History in Blue*
John Rybicki, *Traveling at High Speeds*
Mary Ann Samyn, *Inside the Yellow Dress*
Mark Scott, *Tactile Values*